WHAT YOUR EMPLOYEES CAN'T OR WON'T TELL YOU

WHAT YOUR EMPOYEES CAN'T OR WON'T TELL YOU

Ashley Moyé

No Commission Publishing

Ebook ISBN 9781734723465
Paperback ISBN 9781734723458
Hardback ISBN 9781734723441

Cover design by Ashley Moyé

Publisher's Cataloging-in-Publication data

Names: Moyé, Ashley Ruth, author.
Title: What your employees can't or won't tell you : a handbook
    for C-suite executives on how to improve employee retention /
    Ashley Moyé.
Description: First trade hardback original edition. | No
    Commission Publishing. | Windham, ME, 2023.
Identifiers: LCCN: 2023918402 | ISBN 978-1-734723-44-1
Subjects: LCSH: Business--Management. | Business--Personnel
    management. | Business--Economic aspects. | Executives. |
    Chief executive officers--Salaries, etc. | Business--Costs. |
    Business--Employees. | Business--Labor productivity. |
    Business--Moral and ethical aspects. | Compensation
    management--Handbooks, manuals, etc. | BISAC: BUSINESS
    & ECONOMICS / Leadership. | BUSINESS & ECONOMICS /
    Human Resources & Personnel Management. | BUSINESS &
    ECONOMICS / Labor / General.
Classification: LCC HF5549.5.M64 2023 | DDC 658.4092—am

10 9 8 7 6 5 4 3 2 1

Please direct all inquiries to: editor@nocommissionpublishing.com

"I work to live.
"I don't live to work."
- Anonymous

We are facing a crisis. Generations of workers are barely getting by, and most of them will be forced to work until the day they die. Why?

As a C-suite executive, it's past time you were reminded or called out on what you're doing that is contributing to the degradation of our society's quality of life.

More than likely, the reason why you picked up this handbook was because you're exploring reasons for why your company has trouble recruiting qualified candidates and retaining them. After all, you can't generate top-line growth if you don't have sufficient workers to provide the goods or services that you're selling.

I just love those "team member meetings" that ask the workers to provide feedback to upper management on how to improve the company. What a crock. You know what that sound of crickets means? *I'm not the one making $50,000+ a* *year. Why should I tell you how to do your job?*

Let's harken back to the days of our business administration courses at college. In a nutshell, we were taught how to reduce costs, not break any laws so we don't get arrested/sued, market the product/service, file taxes, and calculate our profit margin. What we weren't taught is how to truly command respect and loyalty from employees, which in turn helps improve the balance sheet's net assets (i.e., they care about the company's success).

If you're too busy to read this entire handbook, skip to the summary on page 35, where I cut to the chase. I can assure you; however, that you will be shocked and will likely toss this handbook aside, because you will not like my answer to fix the fundamental problems that every business faces—be it in the private or government sectors—unless you understand the logic that is contained herein.

Questionnaire One

What is the fundamental reason why you have a job?

_____

_____

_____

How does your home life, and meeting your transportation needs, impact your productivity level at work?

_____

_____

_____

Name your top five priorities in life and number them by ranking:

_____

_____

_____

If you're like most people, the reason why you have a job is to earn a living.

Let's examine that phrase: *earn a living*.

Easily found online, The American Heritage® Dictionary of the English Language, 5th Edition, provides the following definitions:

earn - To acquire or deserve as a result of effort or action.

living - The condition or action of maintaining *life*.

life - The physical, mental, and spiritual experiences that constitute existence.

You are not your employees' therapist. They don't trust you to be that (and likely you don't want to be one). They aren't going to tell you that every day that they have to haul their ass into work, they feel dead. They "hang in there" for the weekend, so they can sleep in, do their laundry, go grocery shopping, clean the place where they live, and hopefully spend some time with their favorite pet or person(s), which just may end up being the equivalent of them watching television or some other form of media that holds the semblance of human interaction. This is, of course, considering that the employee does not have another job or is furthering their education. Summarily, though, they are <u>exhausted</u>.

Do you see what's missing there? Where's the time for *living*? Never mind these people can barely afford rent/a mortgage payment. Where's the time to pursue hobbies, connect with family, volunteer—all the soul-enriching experiences that make life worth living? And, no, they don't have time to do these things during the workweek. Their focus is on getting to work on time: bathed and fed, then getting home in one piece so they can eat dinner (maybe do dishes) and collapse into bed. And, since we now live in a society that mandates a two-income household, too many children are raising themselves.

This is not life. This is legal slavery.

Starting in the mid-1990s, I worked as a

customer service representative at a prominent

mortgage company. I hated my job, but I got

along well with my co-workers. We all hated our

jobs. At the time, I was in my early 30s. Even

though I was capable of handling overtime, when

 it became

available, more

often than not, I

was exhausted

before the end

of my typical eight-hour workday. By the time I

got home, with my 45-minute commute, I only

had enough energy to shove some food into my

mouth and go straight to bed. And a social life? I

didn't have time for much of one.

I was content enough, though, as I was able to buy what I considered my dream car (a

Ford Probe) and I had my own apartment; however, the only reason I could afford those two things was because my mother was my landlord— I had the inside scoop on a low-cost rental with an immediately approved application, and getting a fair deal on my used car sure helped. Although the old four-unit building where I lived was a dump in a crappy neighborhood, it was still safe enough. Keeping my expenses down, I was able to save some money by the end of the month. I considered myself lucky.

Most of my peers had a tougher time of things. What I found most ironic was one young woman's situation, who I'll call "Lisa."

Lisa was married and had one child. Her husband was a construction worker that built houses. I found it incredulously ironic that there was this woman and her husband, who were both helping other people put roofs over their heads, and yet, even with their combined income, they could not qualify for a mortgage (given the market's housing costs within our area).

Beyond that, what really stood out to me the most about working there, was how my co-workers looked at the end of their shift. Most of them looked like they'd been hit by a train. Dazed, exhausted and miserable.

Even so, I stayed there for years. The compensation there was better than most businesses in my area. I gained sufficient experience to become a mentor to new hires, with my eye on being a supervisor. I was a go-to for assistance, and people tended to unload their grievances on me. I was a good listener.

My manager named me and another

woman as "Competency Models" for our division. We were interviewed and profiled by an outside research firm, so our employer could hire people just like us.

My manager and I also had several discussions about my hypothesized Robot Syndrome, and she took great measures to address the cause of that phenomena—you know, when you speak to a customer service representative that says and does the same thing over and over every day? They start to sound like a robot, and sometimes they don't actually hear the customer. They just give a rote response based upon some key words that the customer said.

Of even graver concern is that such workers are also more vulnerable to falling victim to a social engineering attack. *Oops! There go some passwords….*

Honestly, it wasn't your employee's intention to give out such verboten data. Those criminals just know how to take advantage of people's weaknesses!

Chew 'em up and spit 'em out. That's the
perception of many an employer, right? Why
would anyone, in their right mind, want to be
loyal to a company that holds such an outlook to
its "valued team members"? When your lower
management responds to an employee's legitimate
concerns about the negative impact that their job
has on their health, the dismissive response of
"Well, this job isn't for everybody," is akin to
saying: You are easily replaced. You are
disposable. We are a cash-grab operation, and we
don't care about you.

Really? This is why so many frontline
workers piss off your customer. Well, go ahead
and crack that proverbial whip. The accountants
convinced you that you'd be saving money for the
company (increasing the C-suite's bonuses), if you
do "blah." Don't be surprised, though, if some
worker somewhere ends up treating you like

garbage. You know, like a domestic worker that steals from you. Or a reckless driver that cuts you off. Or a customer service representative that doesn't care that your delivery arrived damaged, because the packer deliberately smashed the product before placing it into the shipping box. Or the healthcare worker that's so exhausted they inadvertently administer the incorrect dosage of a prescribed medication. Or the police officer that gave you a hard time….

The poison of discontent spreads like wildfire.

Why all this discontent?

Maybe it's the hours.

True story: On my way home from work—this was before the days when cellphones were commonplace—I noticed an older gentleman on the side of the highway. My first impression of him was that he appeared to be the executive-type, based on his attire and the luxury of his car. He was waving his hands in the air to the drivers passing by. Just before I noticed him, I was grumbling to myself about my crappy job with the crappy pay and my crappy life.

I could have stopped. I almost felt sorry for him, because he appeared to be desperate. But I ultimately didn't, because my primary thought was *it's people like you, who screw over, exploit, and get rich off of people like me.*

Funny, every time I've had car troubles out on the road, I've always received assistance from some middle-class bloke, from helping me to get gas to changing a tire. Didn't need to call anyone.

Poor people take care of their own, I guess.

Overworked and Underpaid

Do you want to pay your employees to be productive and contribute to the company's success, or do you just want to put a warm body there to meet the quota? Of course you want them to be productive. As a leader in your company, it's your obligation to ensure that you not only hire qualified personnel (directly and indirectly), but you create a working environment that is conducive to allowing those hired to be productive. So, what can you do, to ensure that the employee is giving 100%? *Because they're not.*

For decades I've recognized that a human being's productivity level declines over the course of a normal workday. I didn't need any scientific data or peer-reviewed studies to tell me that. I learned an invaluable lesson the day I hit the wall while running laps in junior high school and have carried that lesson with me throughout my entire life.

Human beings produce a finite degree of energy. If they expend more, than they are able to produce, they will give out. This is not just in the physical sense; this is also in the mental sense. I won't bore you with long descriptions about how the body creates ATP (energy) to move muscle tissue and how the brain relies on glucose (sugar) in order to function.

Suffice it to say, workers have been conditioned to pace themselves; otherwise, they wouldn't last the typical eight-hour workday. In other words, much like a sprinter will run farther in five minutes, than a marathon runner will, the worker will produce less per hour than they are capable of, so they don't hit the wall before the end of their shift.

Back at that prominent mortgage company, I had the opportunity to meet a higher-up executive, when he "came down" to meet with the team members of my department. I'll call him "Craig."

Craig and I both smoked cigarettes. While taking a smoke break, I jumped at the opportunity to hold a more confidential and controversial discussion with him about what I felt would be of benefit to the workplace. After all, he had said earlier in the meeting that he wanted to know how things could be improved.

I explained to him of my observations of how frequently my co-workers and I looked/felt as though we'd been hit by a train. I noticed that it was typically around the fifth working hour that I started to feel like I was "done."

"What if," I said to him, "we could have a 30-hour workweek: five days, six hours a day?"

"Well, sure. If someone's willing to work part-time, we could incorporate that work schedule into the program," Craig said, likely knowing what our hourly wages were.

I turned to one of my colleagues and asked

her, "Would you be willing to work a part-time schedule: 30 hours a week?"

"I couldn't afford that," she replied bitterly. "I'm usually looking for overtime!"

"Really?" I said with astonishment, "but, how do you feel after working ten hours?"

"Like I've been hit by a train," she said fearfully.

I looked at Craig, and I immediately knew what he was thinking, because we'd all been there. *A tired employee is not a productive employee*, and a tired employee **makes mistakes**.

Now let's talk about the money. I know you knew this was coming.

If you're like most people, your home life has a significant impact on your productivity level at work. When you get right down to it, unless you want to hire only people that are dependent on someone else (like a teenager), you need to be providing a healthy wage to your workers that is sufficient to accommodate the geographic location's cost of living. Moreover, they're not working for you, just to make you rich, they're investing in themselves; by contributing to your company. Their aim is to ensure their comfort and security in their future retirement. Nobody, that is forced to retire from the workforce, wants to be receiving public assistance when they're in their 80s.

Most people don't want mansions. They don't want expensive, luxury cars. They just want to be comfortable. No one, who is working full-time and penny-pinching, should have to decide between buying a gallon of gasoline or a half-gallon of milk, because there are only five bucks left until payday.

And, they shouldn't have to live like rats, either!

Questionnaire Two

What do you think is a healthy budget?

_____

_____

_____

How do you want your employees to live
and get to work?

_____

_____

_____

Name your company's top five priorities in
how it relates to the communities in which it
conducts business and number them by ranking:

_____

_____

_____

I'm sure you realize that living paycheck to paycheck is not indicative of a healthy budget. Just to make sure we're all on the same page, my rule of thumb for an average worker's healthy budget is as follows:

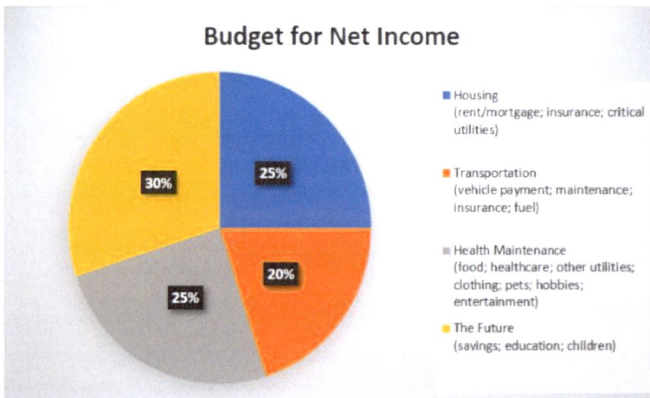

Budget for Net Income

- Housing (rent/mortgage; insurance; critical utilities)
- Transportation (vehicle payment; maintenance; insurance; fuel)
- Health Maintenance (food; healthcare; other utilities; clothing; pets; hobbies; entertainment)
- The Future (savings; education; children)

- 25% of Net income: housing (rent/mortgage; insurance; critical utilities)
- 20% of Net income: transportation (vehicle payment; maintenance; insurance; fuel)
- 25% of Net income: health maintenance (food; healthcare; other utilities; clothing; pets; hobbies; entertainment)
- 30% of Net income: the future (savings; education; children)

Instead of asking your employees to complete yet another survey on how to improve the company, ask your employees how they're living.

<u>Sample Survey Questions</u>

1.) How much is your home's rent/mortgage each month?

2.) Do you share household expenses with anyone? If so, is it by choice or necessity?

3.) Have you ever experienced lack of nourishment since you've been working here?

4.) Has your personal financial stress ever had a negative influence on your workday?

5.) How much money are you able to save each month?

6.) Do you ever worry about your future and the possibility of you being homeless?

If you're like most C-suite executives, you've been living the good life. Maybe you are a rags to riches story. Maybe you were born with a silver spoon. Either way, I'm wagering you're in for a real eye-opener. If you find the results of such a survey to be disconcerting for you, congratulations. You have a heart.

If you don't care and won't even bother to ask them, then, that's why your human resources division has a problem with a revolving door.

What nobody talks about is that too many companies have historically based the calculation of their pay rates on archaic principles. Going back to the days of serfdom, with some adjustments for inflation, the lower echelons of a corporate entity are getting the $haft—just like the peasants did, way back when.

One can't look at what other companies are paying their workers for a comparable position, to determine what HR can get away with. You need to be looking at the housing costs that are within reasonable commuting distance from where your employees will be working.

If you find out that you feel like choking when you take an honest look at those markets, you may consider taking the same approach that companies of yesteryear had to take, when they built affordable subdivisions for their workers.

After all, they were in the middle of nowhere, where there was plenty of cheap land.

This strategy is actually a growing trend. A quick search on the internet demonstrates that companies such as Disney, Google, Cook Medical, and others are doing just that.

And, yes, you're right. It is also likely that once the landlords find out that a major employer in the area is paying higher wages, it's highly probable that those greedy landlords will just jack up their prices, so there's another good reason to build affordable housing for your workers.

Living the Dream

Over the years, since my days at that mortgage company, I've conducted what one could consider ethnological research, and have periodically surveyed my peers. I would ask them if they had the choice of working 40 hours a week or 30 hours a week, which would they prefer?

Interestingly enough, not only was there routinely a resoundingly enthusiastic preference for a 30-hour workweek, but the majority of respondents would want a shorter workday, even if it meant a 6.25% decrease in their income, such as is demonstrated in the examples of Group A and Group B.

Group A

Works 40-hour workweek (five, eight-hour days)
Two, 15-minute paid breaks and an unpaid lunch
Earns $20/hour ($800/week)
Overtime available

<u>Group B</u>

Works 30-hour workweek (five, six-hour days)

Two, 10-minute paid breaks and an unpaid lunch

Earns $25/hour ($750/week)

No overtime—ever, and no moonlighting

I know what you're thinking. *This woman is crazy! She's telling me I have to hire more people and spend tons of money!*

Maybe not.

Hear me out. A sprinter will run farther, than a marathon runner will in five minutes, because the marathon runner has to pace himself. So an employee in 'Group B,' who works fewer hours, will be more productive in one hour, than an employee in 'Group A' will be. It won't be just because the worker in Group B has a greater quality of life, but because the Group B worker will be reward-motivated to perform better.

They'll <u>want</u> to keep that job!

They won't be shirking their job's duties. There won't be any work avoidance strategies.

They're going to be on time, focused and getting the job done. I reckon you'll see those performance statistics trend upward!

To further prove my point, a mason once told me that if he were being paid by the hour, he'd drag that project out as far as he reasonably could; however, when he was working on a similar project that was being paid for on a flat-rate basis, he'd get that job done in less than half the time (compared to the hourly rate project). Summarily, he made more money on the hourly rate project; however, per hour, he made more money on the flat-rate project.

The lessons here are: people are capable of doing more than what you would otherwise expect AND you get what you pay for.

So, what if one employee is actually capable of doing the work of two or even three people? Let's look at the basic math:

If a Group A worker is only able to process 25 widgets per hour on average, yet a Group B worker is able to process 60 widgets per hour on average, then it takes two Group A workers to do about the same amount of work that a Group B worker is capable of.

One (1) Group B worker is paid $750/week.

Two (2) Group A workers are paid $1,600/week.

Do you see the long-term savings?

How the performance statistic translates to each respective position, which is the subject of examination, of course, is up to the managing personnel of each division to sort out.

All that said, in comes the *livability* of that hourly rate, because that Group B worker's rent for a one-bedroom apartment is $1,800/month. You surely don't want that person forced to have a roommate, who could be a potential sociopath that causes your valued worker an extraordinary amount of stress. Right? So, based on the rule of thumb for a healthy budget, the Group B worker should be getting paid $60.00/hour, which is

$1,800/week or $93,600/year.

Before you toss this handbook, just remember, you wanted to know how to improve the percentage of your employee turnover rate, while increasing your revenue.

Reminder: When calculating the long-term savings of improving your employee turnover rate, not only do you need to factor in the costs incurred by having to routinely train new employees, but you also have to factor in the loss of revenue, because a new hire does not have the ability to produce to the degree that an experienced employee does.

Now, compare that appropriately paid Group B worker's annual gross income to the exploited, two Group A workers': $93,600 to $83,200.

The Group B worker's pay raise doesn't seem so bad, now, does it?

Craig balked at my equation.

"Only if everybody else was doing it and it was the only way to attract applicants," he said, seemingly turning pale. "I mean, really. A generous pioneer would have to start that trend," he added, thinking it through, "and they'd have to have a corporation that was so big that everybody else would have to notice AND they'd have to see the positive impact on the balance sheet. It's all about the rate of return, Ashley, because if you're spending more than you were before and not making much more than you were before.... I don't know, the risk of making less would be a catastrophic blunder. Only a CEO could make that call and I can't imagine any CEO would want to put their neck out like that, unless he or she was the owner/majority shareholder, which is rare. In fact, I can't even think of anyone that would fit that profile. CEOs have a fiduciary duty to the shareholders, and if they went out on a limb like that and failed miserably, they just might be facing criminal charges."

"So, it would actually have to be the shareholders that hold a vote about establishing a 30-hour workweek with higher wages?"

"Yeah, however shareholders usually don't care about the little guys. They're like the kings and queens of the kingdom and all they care about is how much the stocks have gone up and/or their dividends."

He must have seen the look of disappointment in my eyes, as he continued, "Don't get me wrong, I would love a 30-hour workweek with a raise, myself. I could finally go see one of my son's soccer games, because right now, by the time I get home, his games are already over," he said with disgust. "It is a great idea and it would definitely improve morale, but I wouldn't want to be the one to try to push it up the line. They'd think I was crazy and I'd probably be fired."

"Okay, so maybe it won't happen here, but

don't you think, overall, people [in society] would be nicer towards one another, if their quality of life were improved?"

"You're an out-of-the-box thinker with a good heart, Ashley. Wish I could do something. If everybody had a work-life balance like that, the world probably **would be** a better place," he said diplomatically, yet with a hint of despondency, as he dropped his cigarette butt onto the ground and crushed it out with his foot. "Thank you for sharing your thoughts with me," he said, then headed back in. "I'll see you inside."

"You're a good man, Charlie Brown!" I told him as he opened the door. At least I got a smile out of him.

Let's envision, for a moment, what sort of applicants would be **wooing** your HR department, once the word got out that they could enjoy a position akin to the previously mentioned Group

B worker that was getting about three times more than what the competition is paying. They are not the transient worker-type.

I see hardworking, stable, intelligent candidates submitting their résumés for consideration. Once hired, not only will they be doing a better job than your current best, but they'll be improving your customers' perception of your company. Now, they're improving the value of your brand. Your customers and would-be customers <u>will</u> take notice.

Do you think your revenue would go up?

More importantly, do you think the **quality of life** would improve in that community?

You've got to spend money to make money.

A happy employee makes a productive employee.

We can't leave it to the government to solve our society's problems. Historically, it has been the entrepreneurs and businesses that have propelled humanity forward.

Try running a pilot program and see how it goes.

Summary

If you don't want transient workers in your company, pay your employees a minimum of four times the average monthly rent for a decent home, in the market where you need your employees to reside, and mandate a 30-hour workweek (five, six-hour days)—no overtime and no moonlighting.

ABOUT THE AUTHOR

Ashley Moyé

Ms. Moyé served as an undercover, deputized FBI agent for over 15 years, during which time she earned an A.S. degree in business administration. She is currently working on her bachelor's degree in dental hygiene, with the intent of starting her own business in the oral health care field.

For more about the author, visit https://ashleymoye.com.

AUTHOR'S NOTE

The Sherman Antitrust Act of 1890

I've heard a rumor that there may be an organization that is bullying companies into doing their bidding, or face being blacklisted from engaging in business with other companies, etc. Here's a gentle reminder of the Sherman Act:

15 U.S. Code § 1 - Trusts, etc., in restraint of trade illegal; penalty

"Every contract, combination in the form of trust or otherwise, or conspiracy, in restraint of trade or commerce among the several States, or with foreign nations, is declared to be illegal. Every person who shall make any contract or engage in any combination or conspiracy hereby declared to be illegal shall be deemed guilty of a felony, and, on conviction thereof, shall be punished by fine not exceeding $100,000,000 if a corporation, or, if any other person, $1,000,000, or by imprisonment not exceeding 10 years, or by both said punishments, in the discretion of the court."

https://www.law.cornell.edu/uscode/text/15/1

In my opinion, I wouldn't trust the swamp's DOJ to do anything about it.

ALSO BY THIS AUTHOR

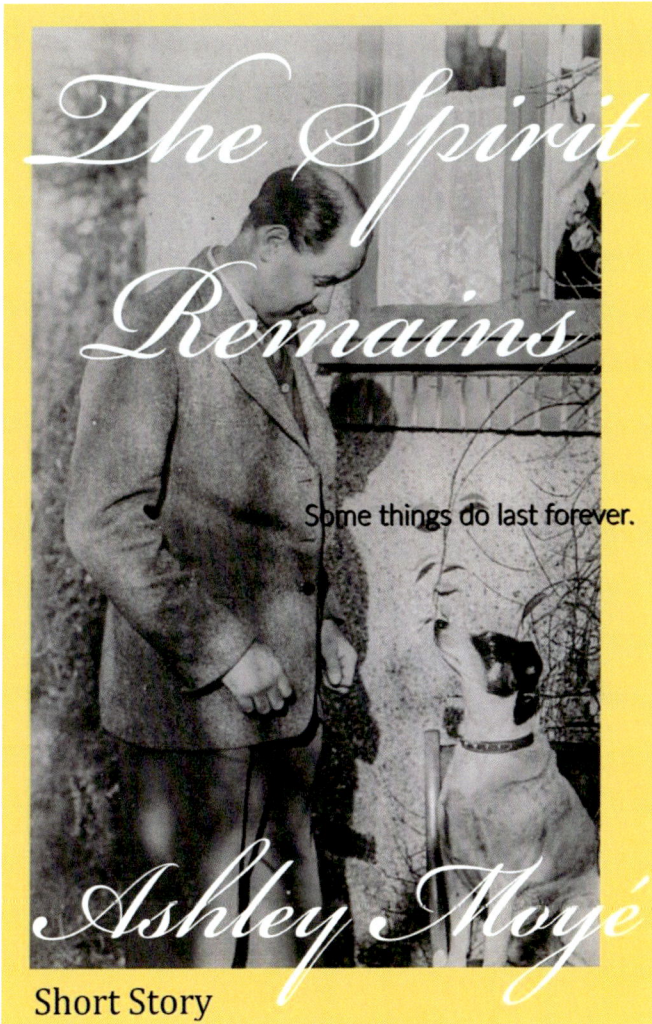

The Spirit Remains

Some things do last forever.

Ashley Moyé

Short Story

ISBN 9781734723434
Ebook ISBN 9781734723403

Coming Soon

Roses Through the Mist

His love was her salvation.

Ashley Moyé

ISBN 9781734723410
Ebook ISBN 9781734723427

NOTES

www.ingramcontent com/pod-product-compliance
Lightning Source LLC
Chambersburg PA
CBRC101601190326
41458CB00033B/6512

The Agile Picture Book

Simon Gibson

Indarien Publishing
www.indarien-publishing.com

Indarien

Mika steps cautiously into the lobby, her heart beating fast.
It is her first day at magnificent Alpha Corp. She gazes
nervously around her new surroundings.

In the corner, Mika spies a group of fresh-looking people. "Are you my manager?" she asks. An intern shakes her head curtly and points at a screen near the elevators.

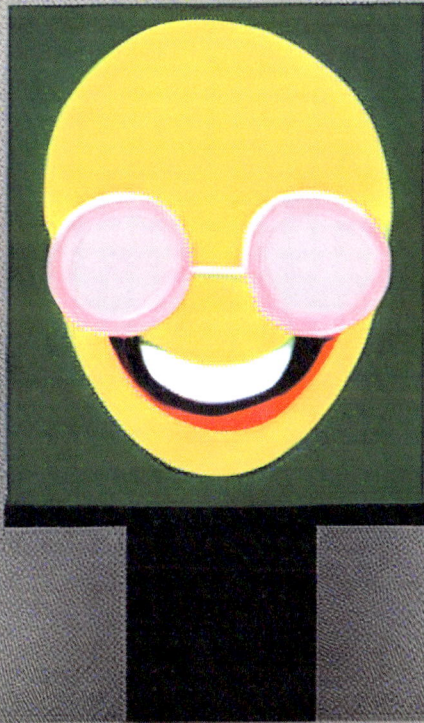

Mika strides across the lobby to the virtual receptionist and enters her name. Flashing on the screen: ID Photo. Human Resource Operations.

Stepping out of the elevator, Mika stalks through the gloom. "Do I get my ID photo taken here?" The wintel engineer shakes his head. "You need security. Carry on down the hall."

Mika hears chanting as she peers into an office. Who is that kneeling in the darkness? Is it security? No, it is a project manager praying to the Gantt Charts. Mika shudders and hurries on.

Mika is startled to see a trio of grey-shirted security consultants flanking a senior manager. They glare at her. Mika steels her resolve. She must be getting closer.

"You must be Mika," says a stern looking figure. He takes her photo with a special device. "Your manager is on level 5," he explains, handing her the still warm card.

Exiting the elevator, Mika walks down an empty corridor. In the distance she hears cheering. It must be her team celebrating. She hurries on excitedly.

The laughter and vibrant voices grow louder. Mika opens a heavy blast-proof door. The Sales Executives are networking feverishly. Mika trades socials.

Glad to escape the frivolity, Mika skips down the hallway and opens another door. She spots movement in the corner. It is a network engineer feverishly pulling cables.

Mika peers through a glass window. She gazes in horror as she watches a tester hammering furiously at her screen, creatively breaking the latest software release. Mika hurries on.

An Environments Manager looks up from soothing the souls of the troubled project managers. "DevOps eh. They have booked level 9 for this sprint." Mika smiles and soldiers on.

Exiting the elevator on level 9, Mika spots a helpful looking application support analyst. "Try the basement. I've heard they are about to go live."

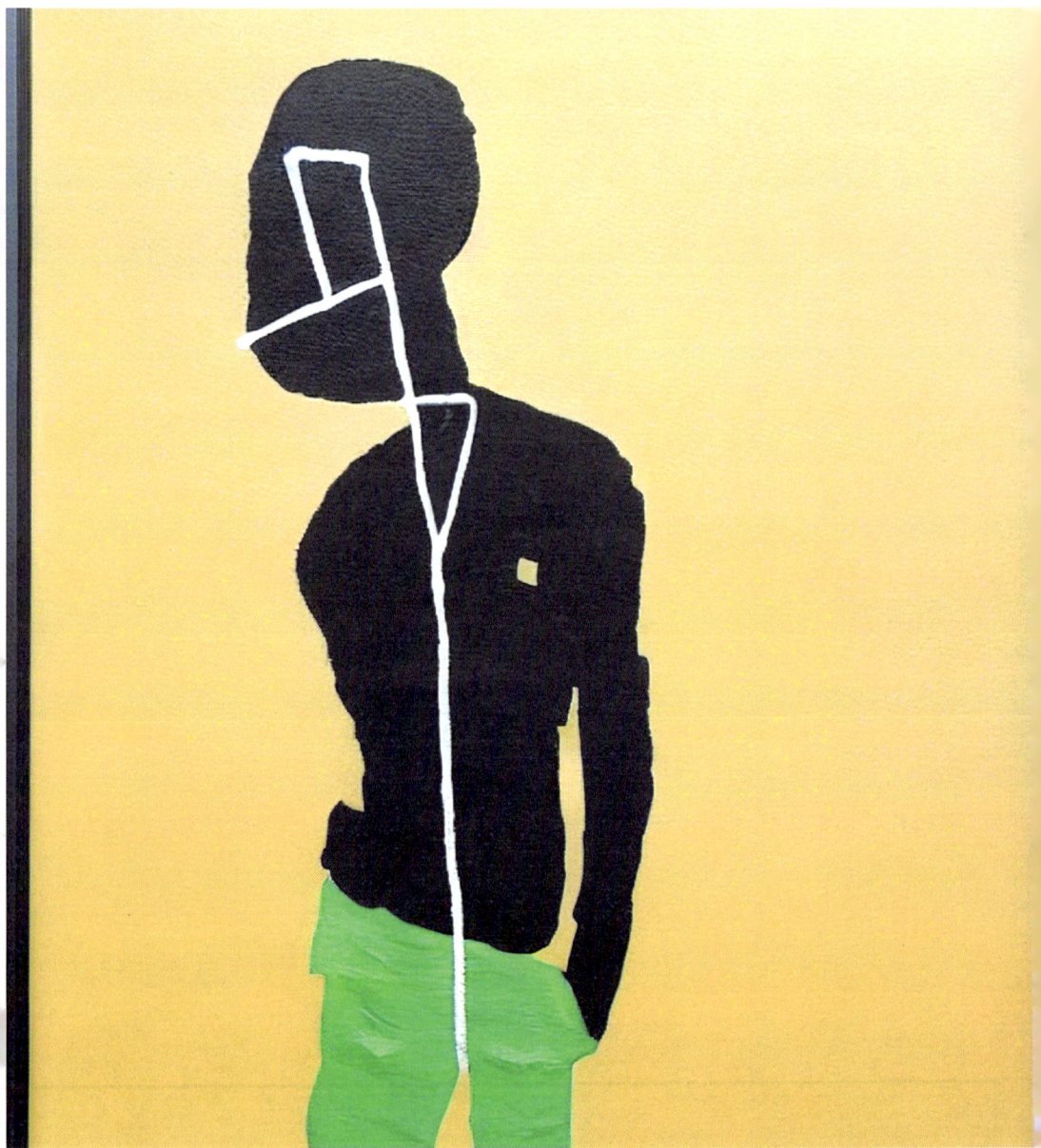

In the elevator, Mika meets a figure dressed in black. It is the CEO. Gathering her courage she says hi. "Hi. I'm off to stock up on some more t-shirts," he replies.

Exiting the elevator, Mika feels the rhythm of tribal music rise from the floor. It is the CIO rehearsing the successful go-live announcement. He waves her down the hall.

"Ah Mika, you must be here about the change," says the Developer. Swiftly, the Developer raises a pull request and goes back to staring out the window.

"Are you sure you should have just dropped that table in production?" says an DBA. The reply - "Don't worry, pretty sure we have some backups on tape" - has Mika running.

A well dressed young man gesticulates fervently. Is it a DevOps engineer? No, it is a Data Scientist untangling a spiders web of R package interdependencies.

A scrum master waits in a room liberally festooned with post-it notes. She looks Mika straight in the eye and says, "Go to the sixth floor. The Change Manager is waiting."

"Ah, you must be Mika," says the Change Manager.
Screens flicker in the haze. "The change is stuck at
approvals. Go forth and get authorization." Mika groans.

Chasing approvals, Mika runs from cubicle to server room to office to meeting room. Down crowded corridors and up flights of stairs. Finally the change is approved.

"Congratulations, the change is approved." The Release Manager presses a large green "Go Live" button. Moments later Mika hears a hiss in the distance and then a loud bang.

Mika descends into the depths. A strange figure hovers above the floor. Lights flash. She smells ozone. The walls quiver as a blast goes off in the distance. She sprints.

A wounded Platform Engineer stumbles into view. He staggers, and Mika catches him. "It's alive," he mumbles, barely coherent. "Roll it back," he gasps.

Mika runs into a SRE. "The platform is under attack. We need to roll back the change." The SRE scoops up her docking station. They dash towards the core of chaos.

Entering the last office Mika is greeted by the howls from the project team. A figure in black suit raises his arms pleadingly. As the light flickers he croaks, "Save us."

Mika locks in, brushes off the blowfish algorithm and deploys the fix. Fans whirr and the scream of tearing metal rises to a peak and then dies away in the data center.

A hatch in the ceiling slowly opens. Mika ascends.
Who are these people on the roof chasing butterflies? Mika
smiles. She has found her tribe.

A big thanks to Cam Hart, Nick Aarts, Paul W., CollisLy, BC, AK, Huw and Hiwada-san, Greg M., Jim and Andrew, Bhaskar and Shail, TC, CJ and CD.

This book started as a bit of fun, playing with Stable Diffusion and pytorch to see what could be created. Images were generated on a humble home PC running Debian GNU/Linux 12 (bookworm) with a NVIDIA GeForce GTX 3060 video card. The training data was v2-1_768-ema-pruned.ckpt, licensed under a CreativeML Open RAIL-M License. Over 3000 images were created for this book. Using AI makes the process curatorial and a specific aim was not to obfuscate the use of AI technology.

Book design by Indarien Ltd.
ISBN 978-0-473-74248-5

Published by Indarien Limited
www.indarien-publishing.com
Copyright © 2025 Indarien Limited